HOW PEOPLE EARN AND USE MONEY

By Muriel Stanek

Pictures—Jack Faulkner

BENEFIC PRESS · CHICAGO

Primary Supplementary

Social Studies Program

How Series

HOW HOSPITALS HELP US

HOW SCHOOLS HELP US

HOW WE CELEBRATE OUR SPRING HOLIDAYS

HOW WE GET OUR MAIL

HOW WEATHER AFFECTS US

HOW FAMILIES LIVE TOGETHER

HOW DOCTORS HELP US

HOW AIRPLANES HELP US

HOW WE CELEBRATE OUR FALL HOLIDAYS

HOW WE GET OUR CLOTHING

HOW WE TRAVEL ON WATER

HOW FOODS ARE PRESERVED

HOW WE GET OUR DAIRY FOODS

HOW WE USE MAPS AND GLOBES

HOW WE GET OUR CLOTH

HOW WE GET OUR SHELTER

HOW WE TRAVEL ON LAND

HOW PEOPLE LIVE IN THE BIG CITY

HOW COMMUNICATION HELPS US

HOW PRINTING HELPS US

HOW PEOPLE EARN AND USE MONEY

Photographs furnished by:

Bureau of Engraving and Printing
Bureau of the Mint
John Gorecki
United Press International Photos

Library of Congress
Number 67-12658

CONTENTS

WE NEED MONEY

We use money every day.

We earn money.

4

We spend money.

We save money.

We give it to others.

6

Why do families need money?

Families all over the world need money to buy many things.

They need a place in which to live.

They need food to eat and clothes to wear, too.

The way they get these things is to buy them.

7

Families want other things, too.

They get these things by buying them, too.
All of these things are called goods.

8

Families need
the help that
other people can
give them.

The help each of these people gives is called
a service. Families pay these people for their
services, too.

Why do people today
use money?

A long, long time ago people
did not use money.

When a man wanted something some other person
had, he could get it by working for that person. He
could also give that person something he had for
the thing he wanted.

Today people use money
to buy goods and services.

People today like to
use money. They use money
because it can be carried.

Money can be saved, too.
We don't always spend all
of the money we earn.
Sometimes we save a part of it and spend it later.
We might save all summer to buy a winter coat.

We might save a long time to buy
something that costs much money.

Today we might buy this.

But we might wait until next year to buy this.

WE CAN COUNT OUR MONEY

How does our money look?

All of these coins are money.
They are made of metal.

Half-dollar

Nickel

Dime

Penny

Quarter

Some coins are made
of two kinds of metal.

Where do we get our money?

The United States makes
coins in three places.
Coins are made in
Philadelphia, Pennsylvania.

The coins are inspected
as they are made.

This is the Mint in Denver, Colorado.

Coins are made in San Francisco, and they are also made in Denver.

Silver is kept here
until it is used in making
the half-dollar.

This is the Silver Repository
in West Point, New Jersey.

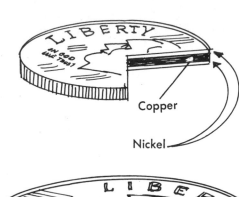

Copper

Nickel

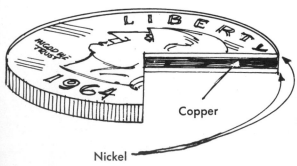

Copper

Nickel

Silver was used to make
dimes and quarters. It is
no longer used to make
these coins. Now other
metals are used in dimes
and quarters.

16

A large number of coins could be heavy to carry. Paper money is not so hard to carry and to count.

The United States Treasury Department makes our paper money. It is made in the Bureau of Engraving and Printing.

Every bill is closely inspected after it is printed.

How many coins is a dollar worth?

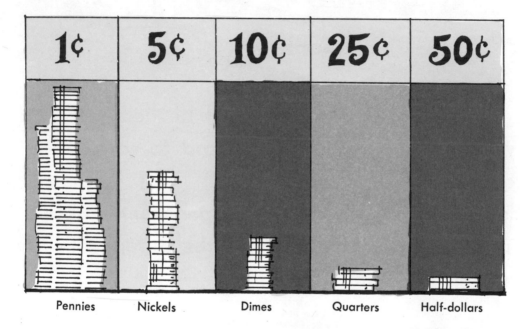

How many pennies are in one dollar?
How many nickels are in one dollar?
How many dimes are in one dollar?
How many quarters are in one dollar?
How many half-dollars are in one dollar?

What is a check?

People do not always pay for things with coins and paper money. If a person wants to pay for something by check, he writes to his bank on paper that his bank gave him. This paper, which is a check, tells the bank to pay the money to the person who is named on the check.

A person may not write a check for more money than he has put in the bank.

WE EARN THE MONEY WE NEED

We work to earn money to buy the things we need. If we do not work, we will not have money to buy these things.

Most people are paid money by other people for the work they do.

Some people work in their own business. The man who owns the business keeps some of the money the business makes.

20

What kinds of jobs do people have?

People work at many kinds of jobs to earn money.

Children can earn money, too. They work after school and in the summer.

They work at home.

They work for people who live near them.

They work near their own homes.

Who are producers?

People who make goods for others to buy are producers. They earn money by selling their goods.

These are some producers of goods.

Farmer

Baker

Dressmaker

23

Window washer   Doctor   Taxi-cab driver

People also earn money for doing services. Here are some producers of services.

You are a producer of goods when you do this.

You are doing a service when you do this.

WE SPEND MONEY

We spend money for goods and services we need everyday. But we spend money for other things, too.

We spend money for fun.

What do people buy?

People buy goods
they can see.

They buy goods
they can touch

and goods they can taste.

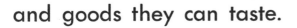

Everything we buy costs something.

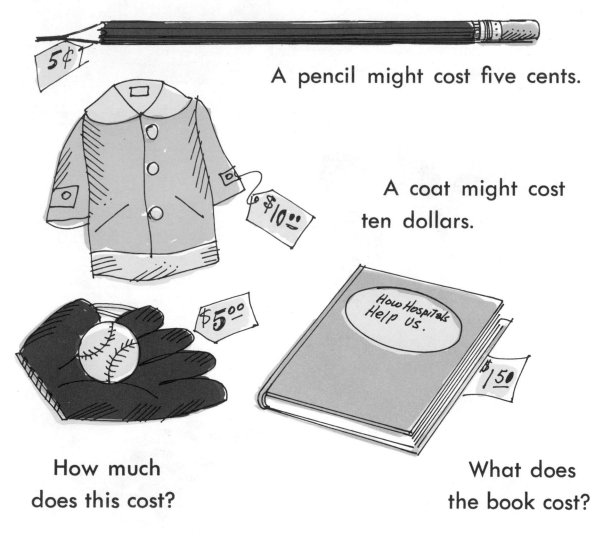

A pencil might cost five cents.

A coat might cost
ten dollars.

How much
does this cost?

What does
the book cost?

If a person earns
ten dollars he
could buy this.

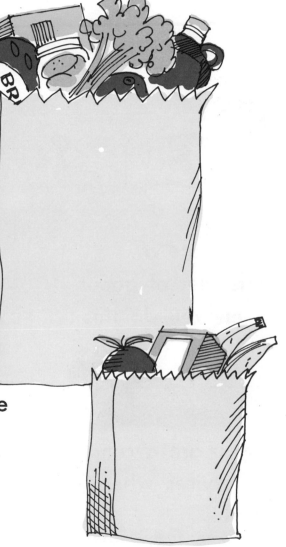

If a person earns only five
dollars he could buy this.

What is a consumer?

A consumer is a person who uses a service or uses goods.

You are a
consumer of goods
when you do this

or this.

You are a consumer
of services when you
do this

or this.

What is credit?

Sometimes people don't have all the money they need to pay for things they buy. The store may let them buy the goods on credit. When a person buys on credit, the man who owns the store will let him pay for the goods a little at a time.

If a man buys a car on credit, he may pay for it a little at a time until there is no more to pay.

But he has to pay more when he buys on credit. The longer it takes him to pay for what he bought, the more he will have to pay.

Before spending money a person should be sure
he is doing the right thing. He should ask:

"Should I spend this money?

Should I save it?

Am I buying wisely?"

THE VALUE OF GOODS

How should we buy?

Money can be used to show the value of goods and services. We can tell the value of goods by looking at them closely. We can look to see if

something is made well. We can see if what it is made of is good.

The money the store asks people to pay is put on the things the store wants to sell.

Goods that have a high value may have a high cost. The cost should be low if the value is low. Looking for the value of goods helps to tell us if it is wise to buy it. We want to get the most for our money.

34

    Before he buys a pencil, this boy
will want to think about these things:
Is this pencil worth five cents?
Can this same pencil be bought for
four cents at some other store?
Would a pencil costing six cents be
worth more than the ones costing
four cents and five cents?

What makes the cost change?

Sometimes the cost of goods goes up when many people want to buy them.

An umbrella might cost more when it rains than when it is sunny.

Bathing suits bought at the end of the summer might cost less than they did when the summer began.

There are many flowers here. That is why the flowers here cost less.

There are not many flowers here. That is why the flowers here cost more to buy.

Why do apples cost more in one place than they do in the other?

WE SAVE MONEY

Many families save some of their money.

Why do people save?

They save money for things they need and want. They may save to buy something big.

They may save so that when they are old they will not have to work hard.

How do people save money?

People may save in different ways.

Some people save money in their cookie jars.

Some save in toy banks.

Many people save their money in a big bank.

Why should we save in a big bank?

The bank is a safe and wise place to save money. Money is safe in a bank because there are men there to keep it safe. Money in the bank will not be lost or burned.

40

It is wise to save in the bank. The bank pays you money that is called interest. When you save your money in the bank, you let the bank use your money to earn more money. This is why the bank can pay interest for money you save in the bank.

The bank may pay four cents interest to a person for every dollar of his it used for one year.

If a person saves ten dollars for a year, he will have $10.40 at the end of the year.

What are savings bonds?

There are other places and ways to save money, too. Money may be saved in savings bonds. A business or the United States government may put out bonds for people to buy. The business or government will do this when it needs money. When a person buys a bond, he is giving the government or business some of his money to use.

The business or government uses the money for a set time. At the end of this time, the person who bought the bonds will get his money back.

These bonds pay interest, too. United States Savings Bonds pay all the interest at one time. The interest is paid at the end of the set number of years.

How can we save money by buying shares of stocks?

Money may be used to buy stocks. Stocks let many people own a share of a big business.

Stocks pay money to everyone who owns a share of the business.

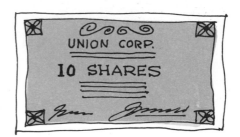

It is hard to save money. But even a little money saved each week grows into more money.

WE CAN USE OUR MONEY WISELY

What is a budget?

A plan for spending and saving money helps people. This plan is called a budget. In a budget, a person writes down all the things he must buy. He also writes down how much money he has to spend. Then he writes down how much he can spend for each thing he has on his budget.

FAMILY BUDGET PER MONTH

RENT	$90.00
FOOD	$80.00
CLOTHING	$40.00
MISC. (DOCTOR, ETC)	$20.00
SAVINGS	$20.00

CHILD'S BUDGET PER WEEK

Notebook paper	10¢
Ice cream + candy	5¢
Savings	5¢

45

Sometimes a budget will help to show the person where he is spending too much money on something. A budget helps people spend their money wisely.

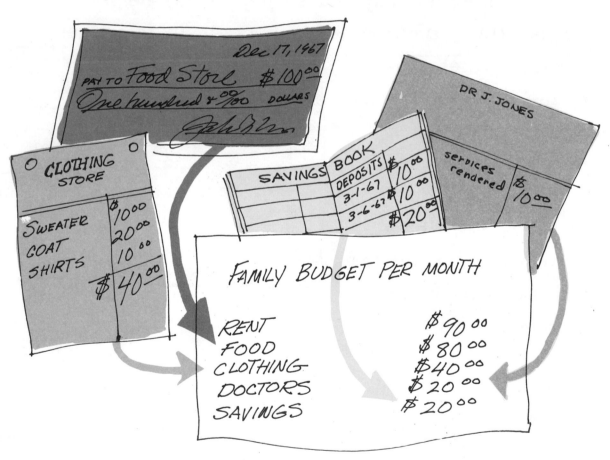

We use money wisely not only when we make
a budget. We also use it wisely when we look for
values, when we buy United Savings Bonds, or
when we buy stocks. We use money wisely when
we save a part of everything that is earned.

Vocabulary

The total number of different words in this book is 240. The 14 words in roman type would be familiar to children reading at the third-grade level. The 11 words in italics are above third-grade level. The rest of the words used in the book are below third-grade level. The number after each word indicates the page on which it first appears.

bonds 42
budget 45
business 20

check 19
coins 13
consumer 30
costs 12
credit 31

dime 16
dollar 18

earn 5

interest 41

jobs 21

less 36

metal 13

nickels 18

pencil 28

person 10
producers 23

quarter 16

service 9
share 44
stocks 44

value 34

worth 18